MW00574922

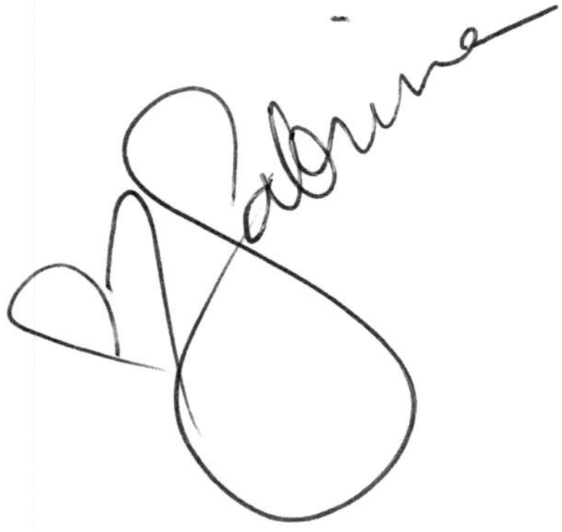
Sabine

# SWIPING FOR

*Prince Charming*

## A Modern-Day Fairy Tale

Text & Creative Direction by Sabrina Marzaro
Illustrations by Merakilya

ISBN: 978-0-578-54765-7

Disclaimer: This story and its characters are entirely fictional. Any resemblance to persons living or dead is completely coincidental. Additionally, certain institutions, places, companies or products may be mentioned, though this book is not affiliated with, or endorsed by them. The author simply has a genuine appreciation for Netflix and certain Parisian addresses.

To all the men that ever

made me stumble…


And the women who helped

me get back up again.


Thank you for helping

me discover my strength.

# Once Upon
## A TIME ...

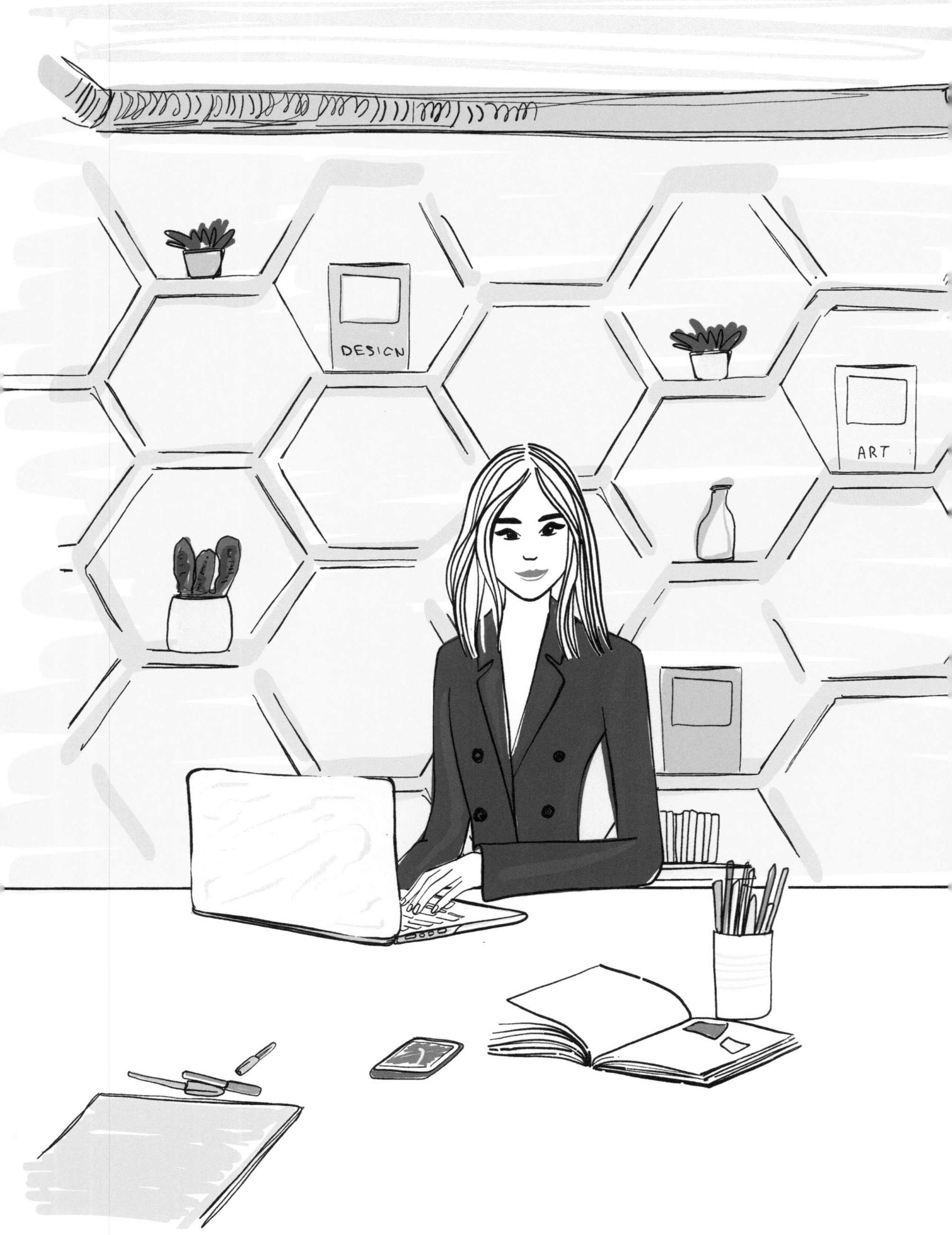
DESIGN
ART

You're a fabulous woman,
pretty, hardworking and bright.
Your career's well underway…
Now, time to find Mr. Right!

You round up your friends
and try to lay down a plan:
"I'm on the search for my soulmate;
could you give a girl a hand?"

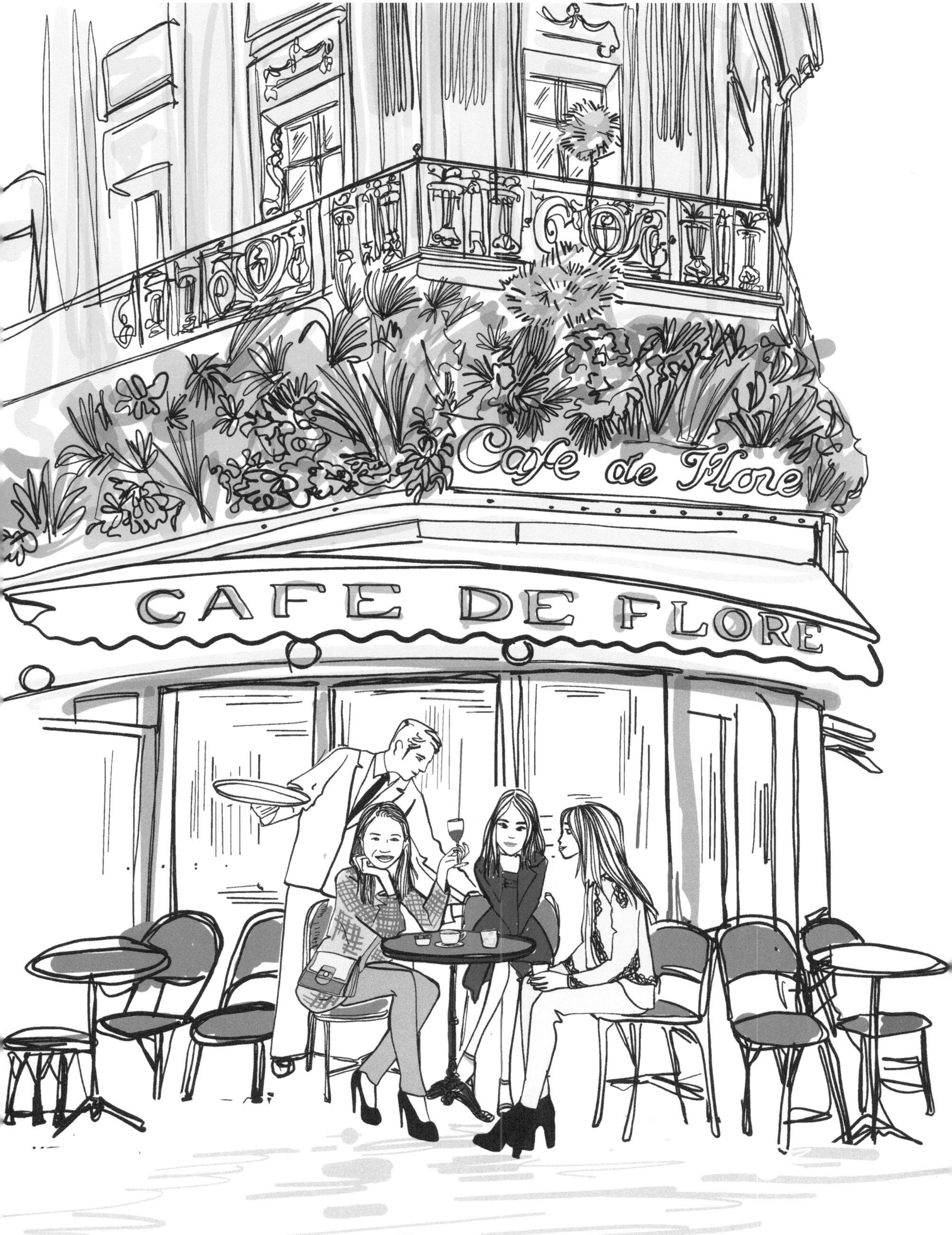
Cafe de Flore
CAFE DE FLORE

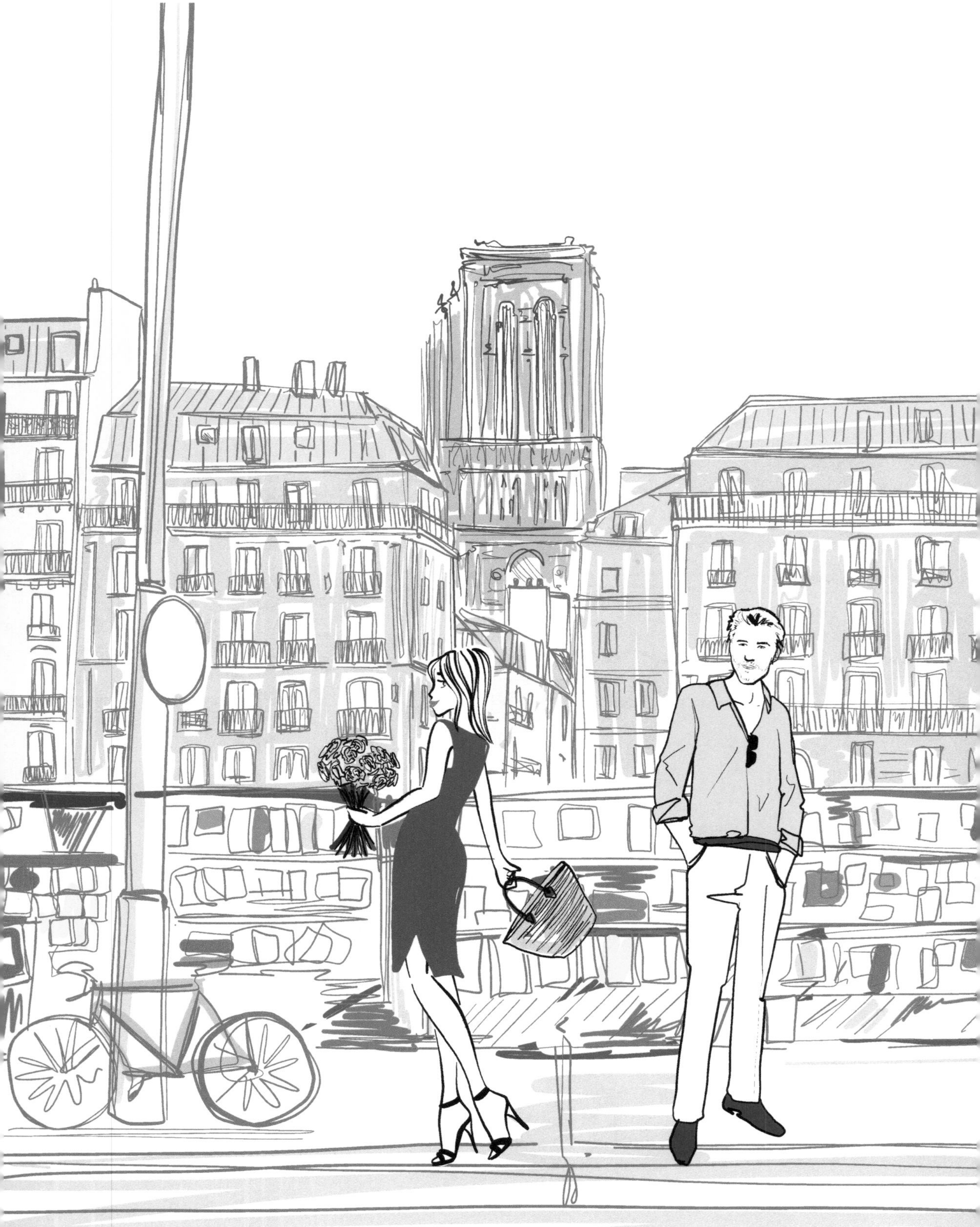

You've sought him out at parties,

hoped to cross paths on the street,

but for some very odd reason,

the universe has yet to let you meet.

So during an evening of Netflix

– when you're at home with your cat –

you finally give in and download an app.

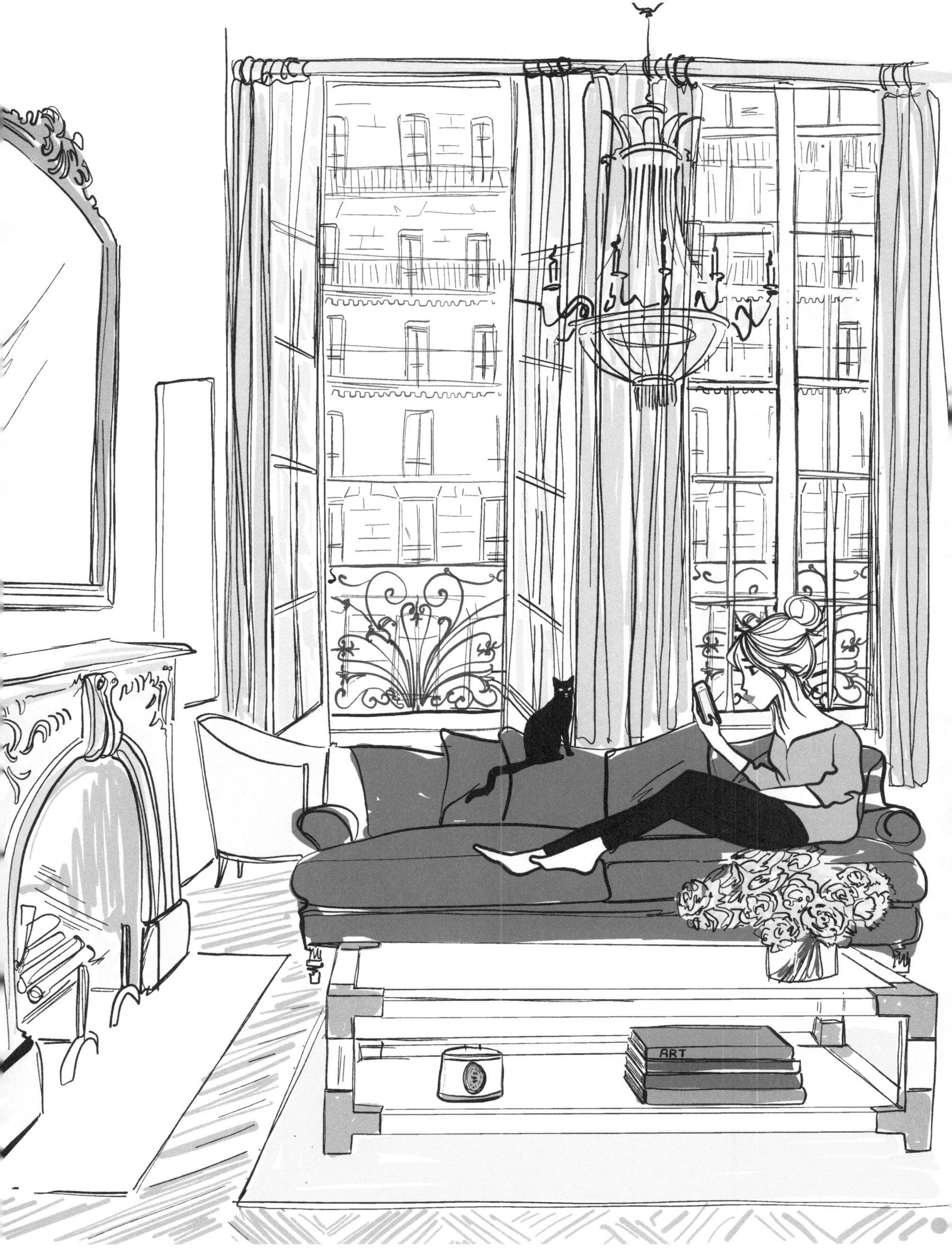
ART

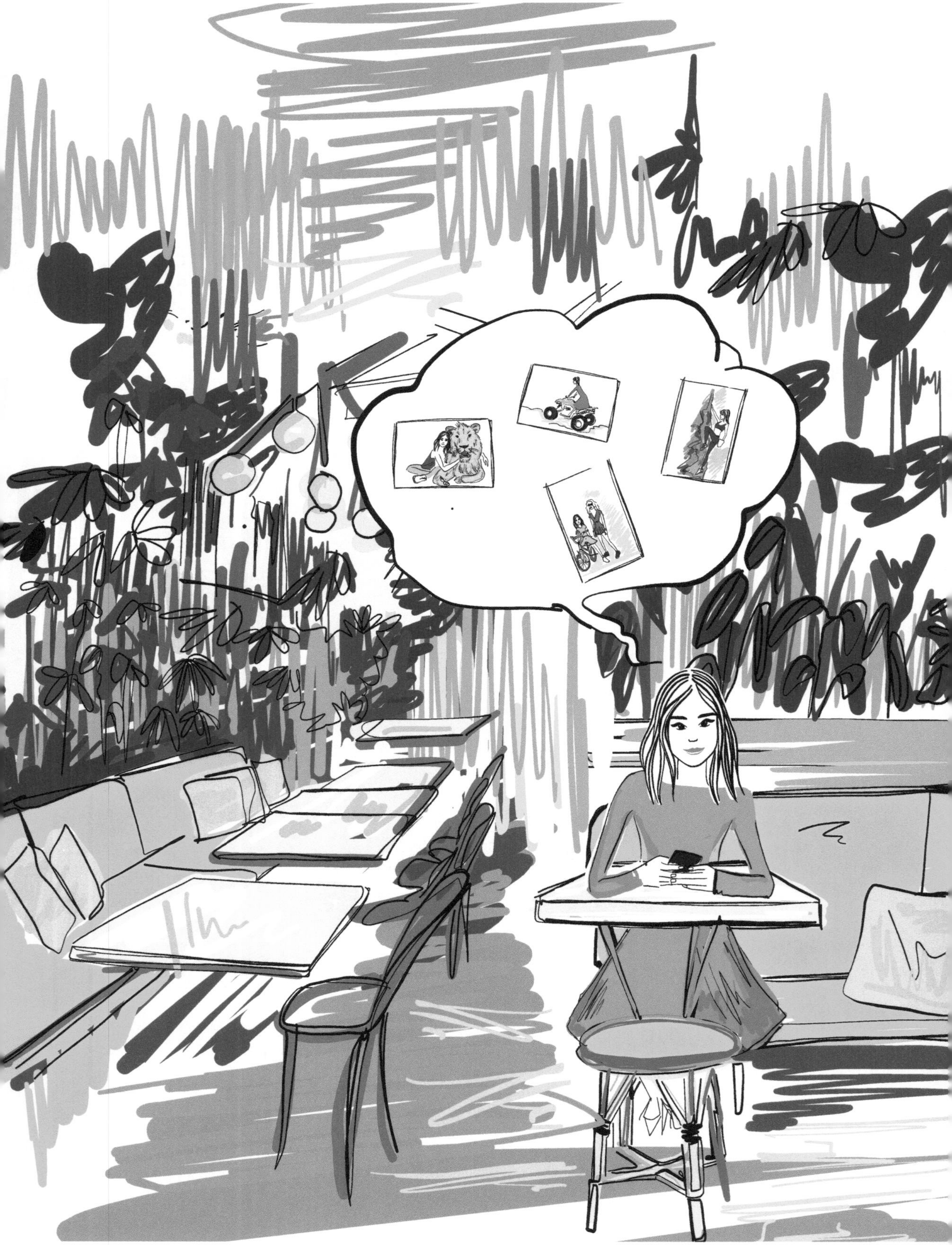

You pick out the photos that

showcase your best traits:

your adventurous spirit,

your impeccable taste.

The moment's finally arrived

for you to see what's in store.

The apprehension builds…

Will you find what you're looking for?

As you continue to swipe,

a thousand lefts, a few rights,

there'll be some days of frustration…

But others of joy and anticipation!

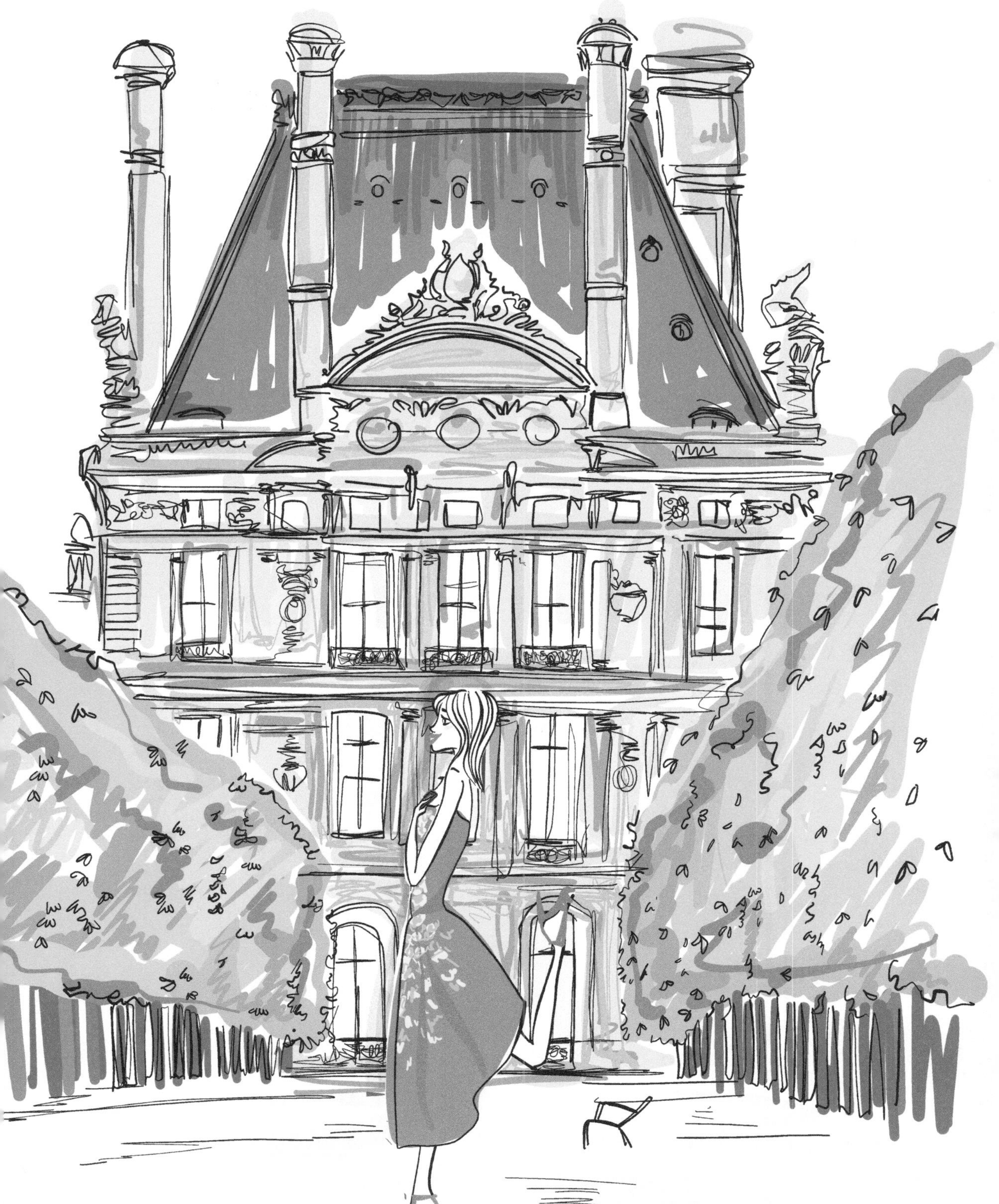

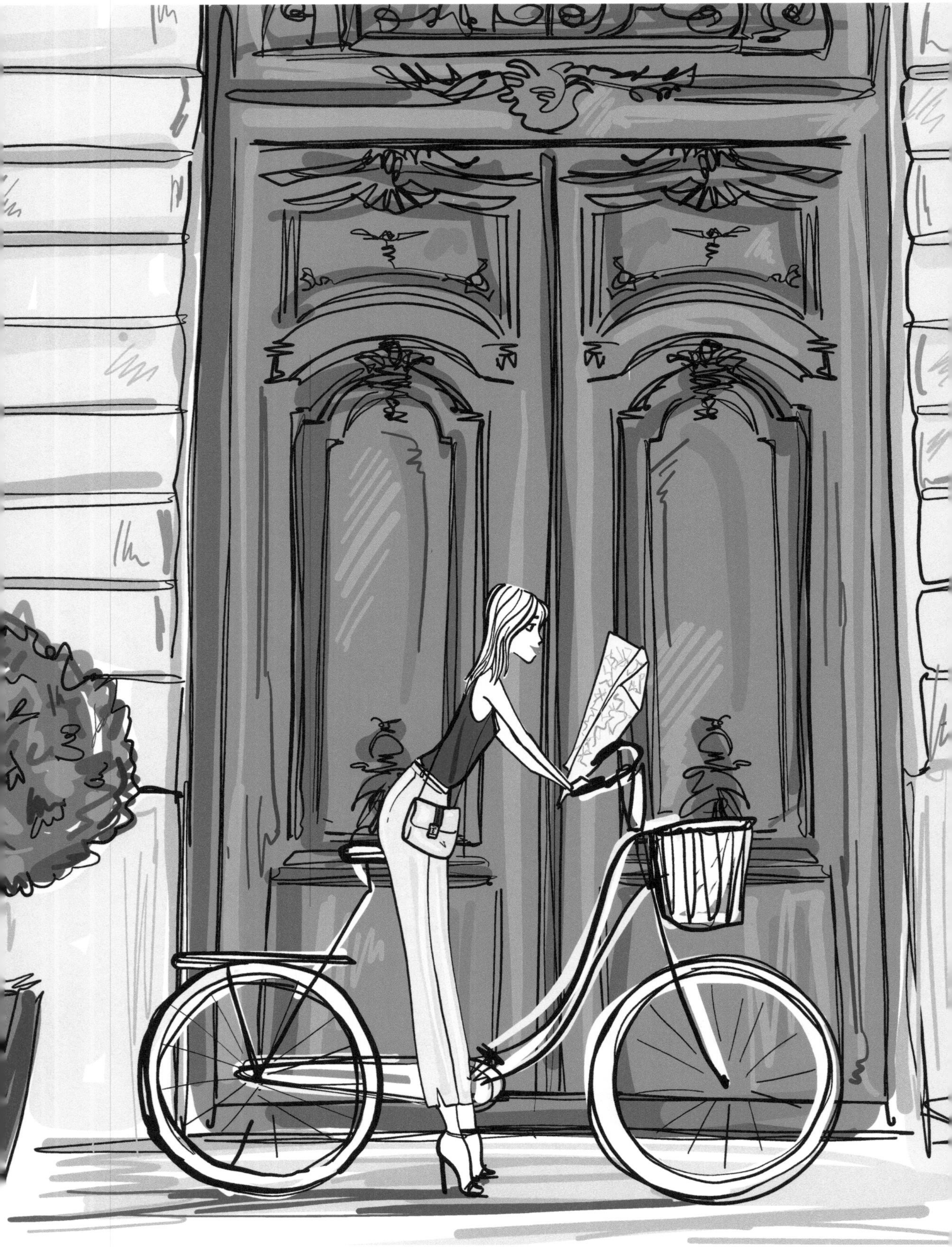

You're taking control of your life
in the search for your man,
and you're willing to seek him out
wherever you can!

You'll meet some that are charming,

certain men that are small,

ones fun and full of wit,

others, like talking to a wall...

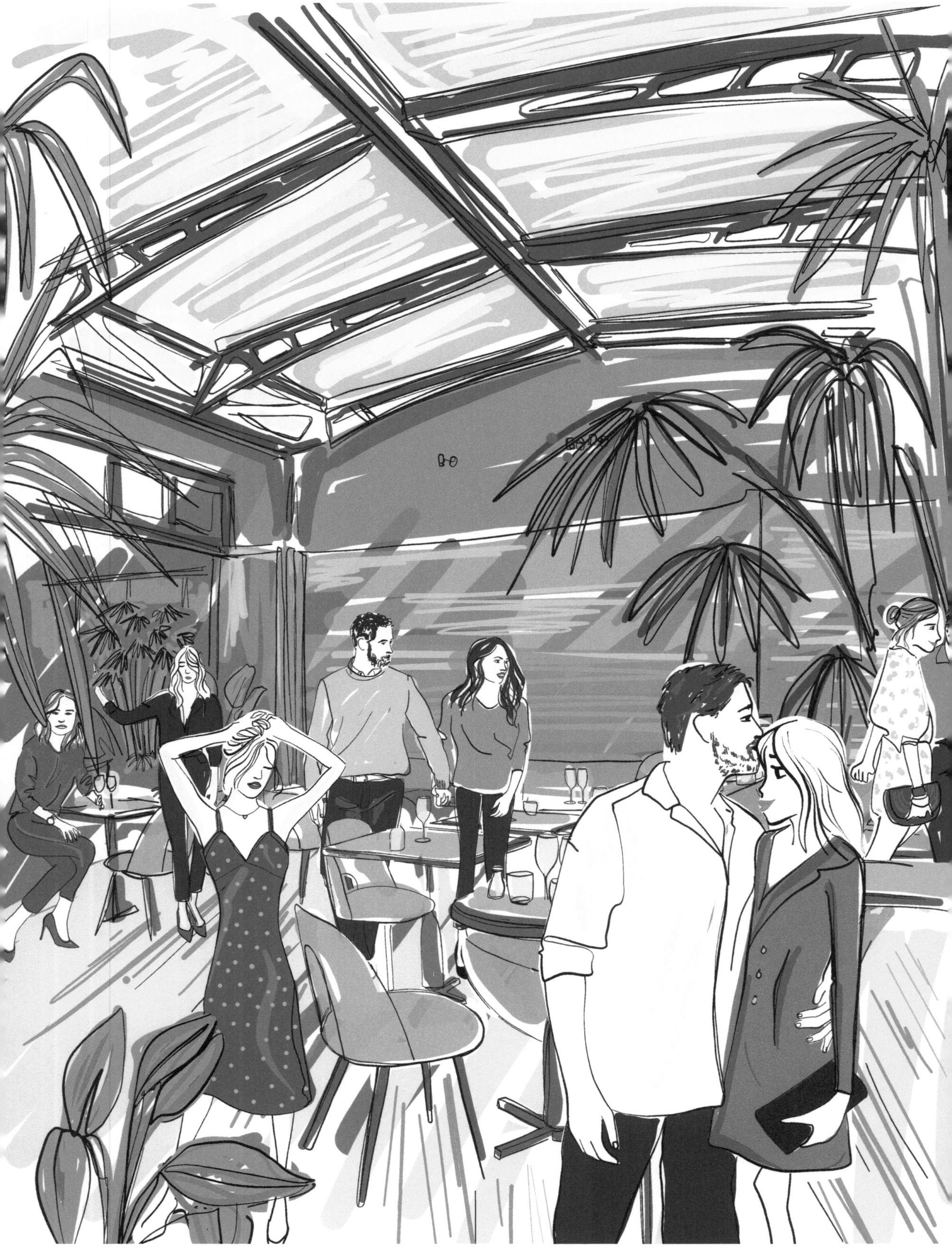

You'll enjoy drinks at cool places,

or strolls through the park…

The first time he holds your hand,

or a kiss that brings a spark.

A first date, then a second…

This one seems like a catch!

If a third date ensues,

he may even be your perfect match!

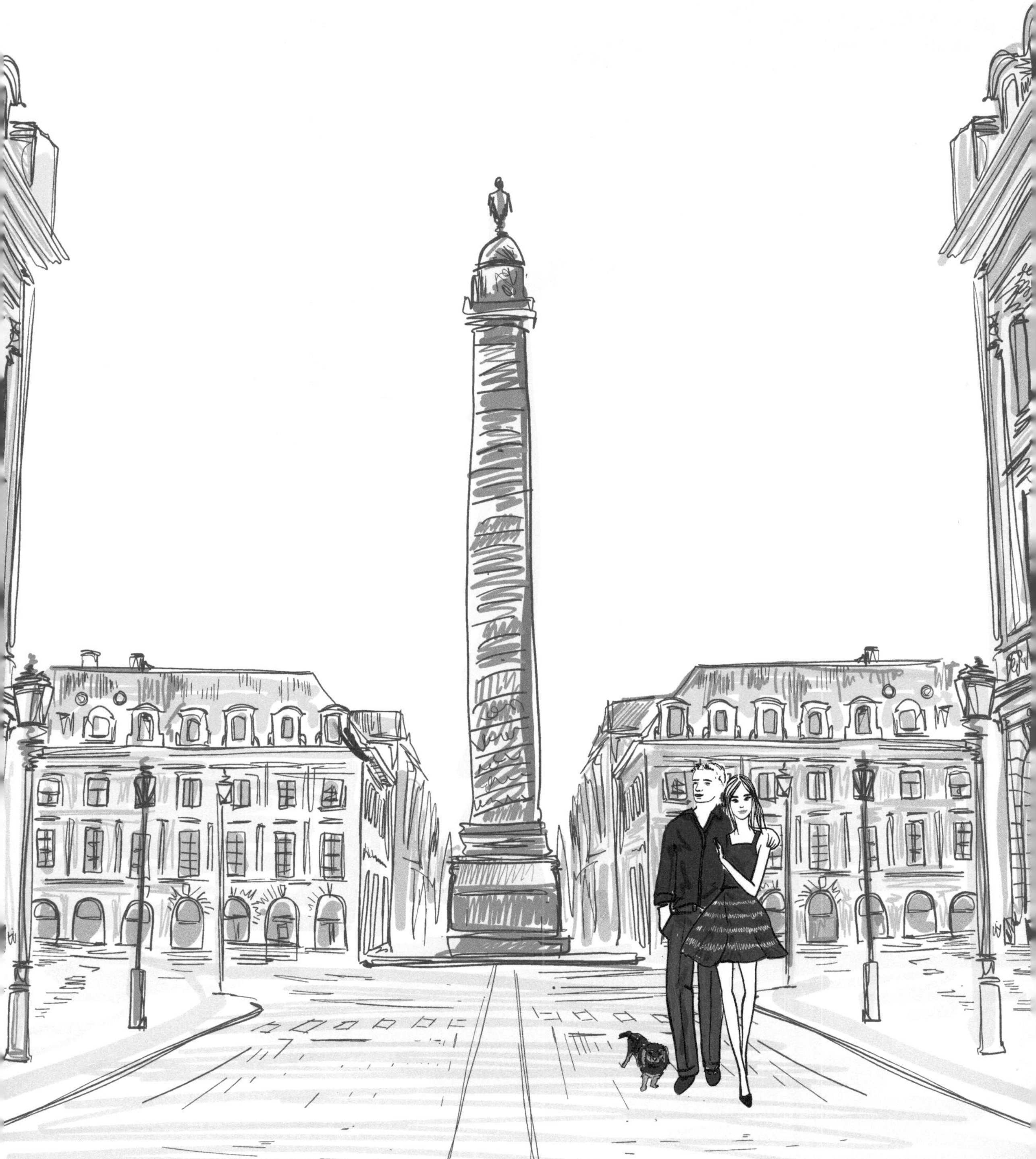

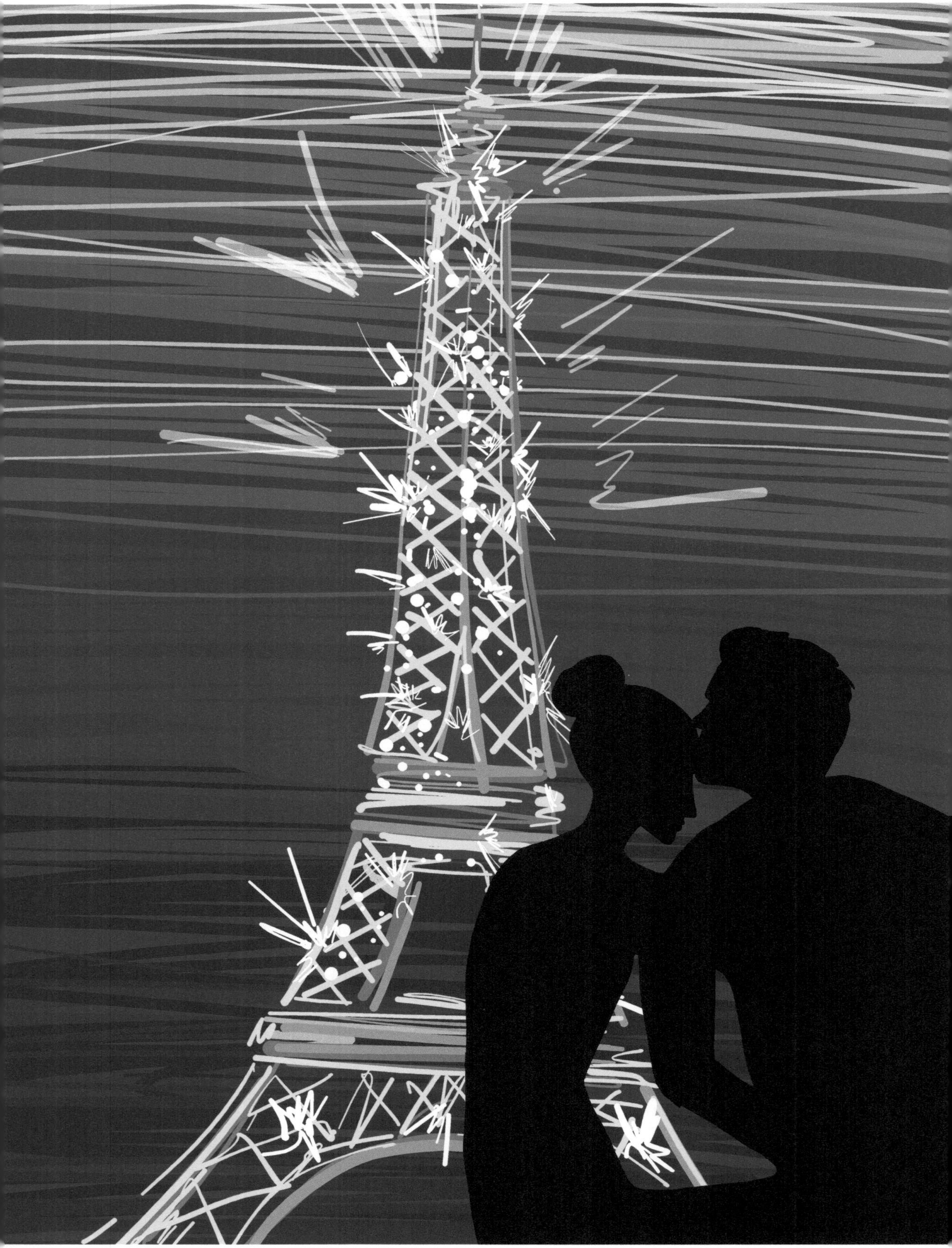

You'll be whisked off on grand adventures,

"the stuff of films" one might say,

and you'll always have great content

to share in the group chat, end-of-day.

First comes the tan Italian

with his high-powered bike.

He'll take you for a spin

to see the city's dazzling lights.

Romantic and magical,

it'll leave you weak in the knees...

Until you come to realize: he's kind of a sleaze.

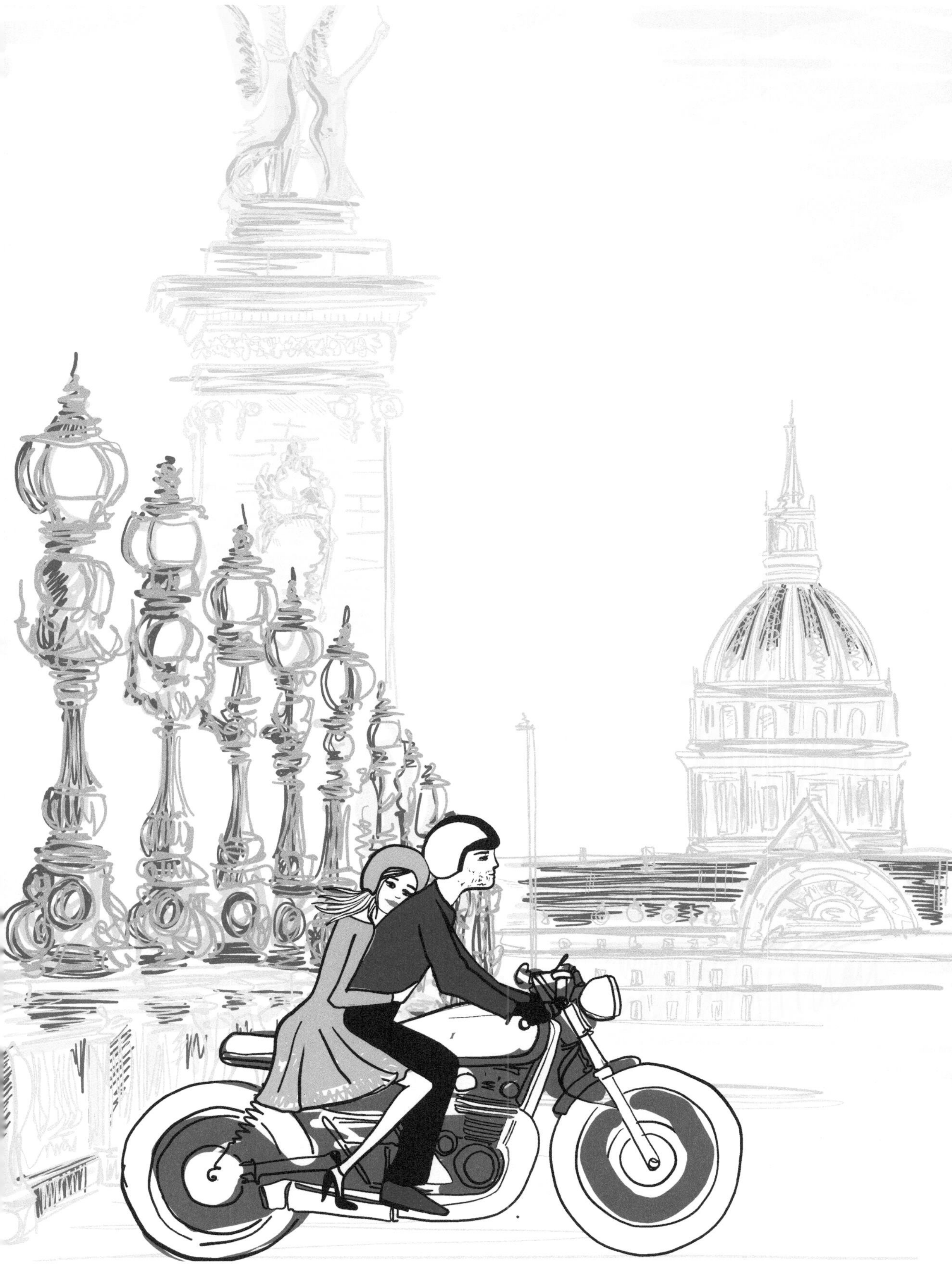

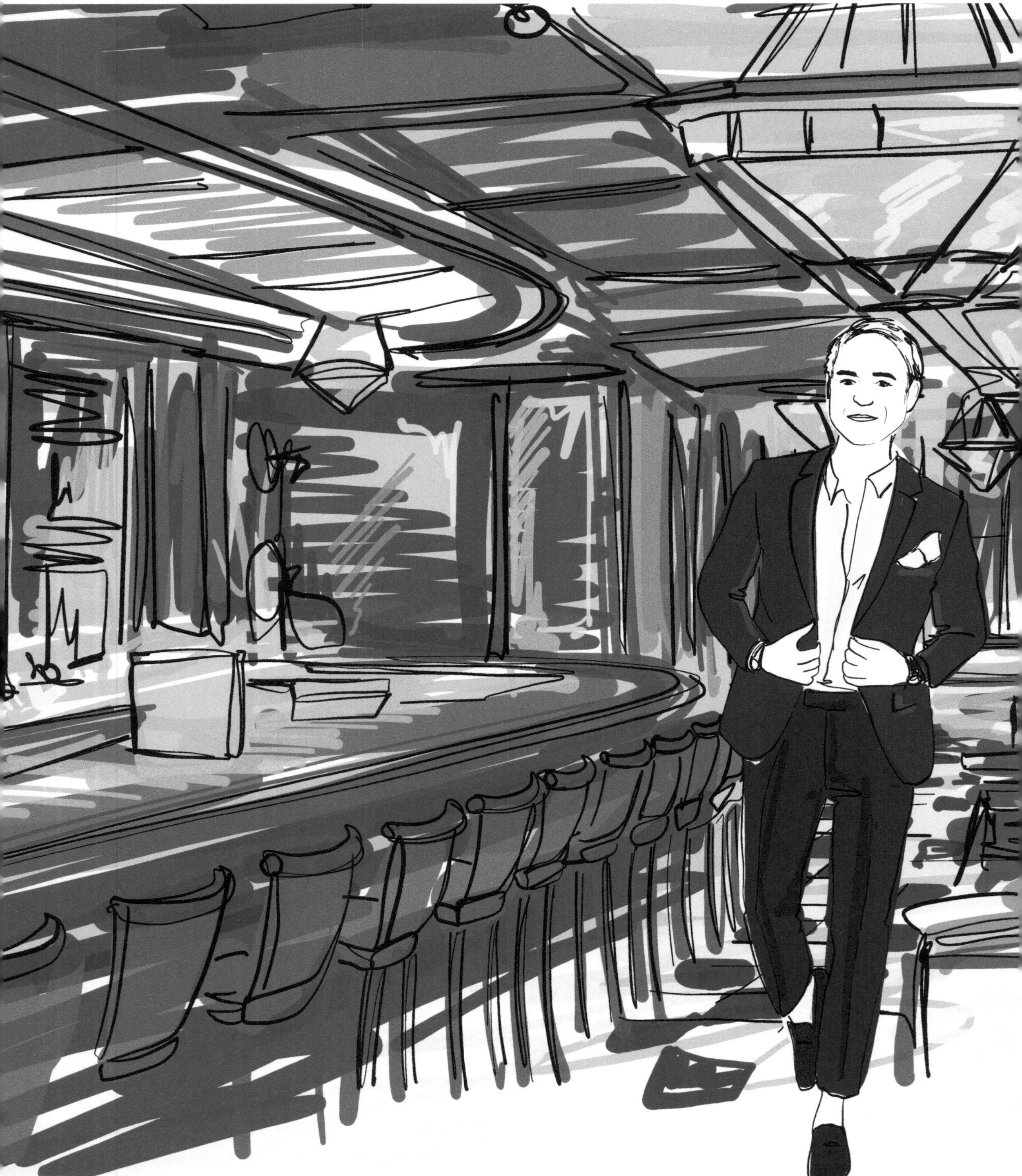

"Now, this one's in finance
and always dressed to the nines.
He's funny and playful;
knows how to have a good time!
But he's suddenly stopped texting
after 4 really great dates.
I guess a true relationship
just wasn't our fate."

"There's this sweet engineer,

who designs high-speed jets!

Kind and attentive –

as good as it gets!

But something feels off,

I really have to attest."

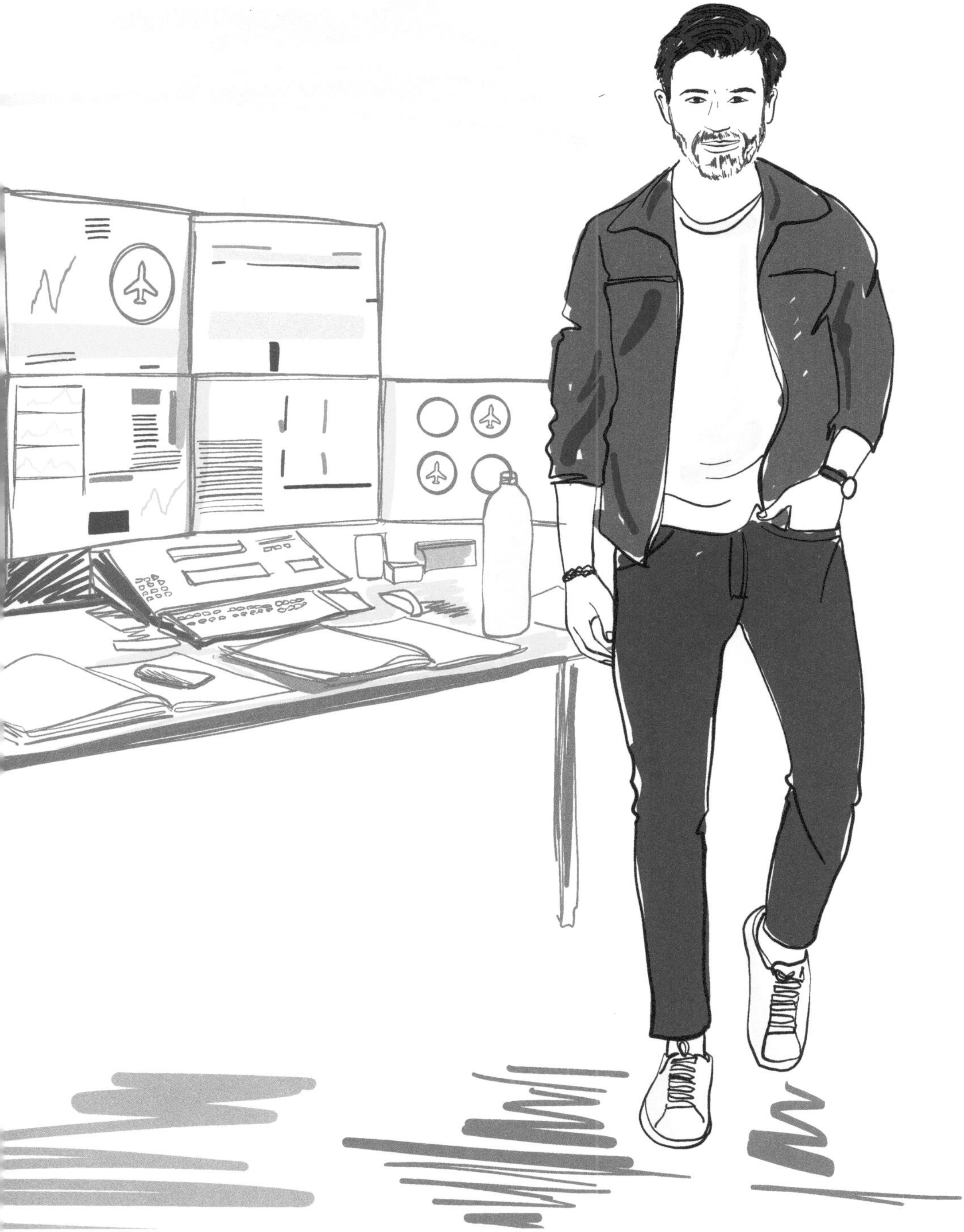

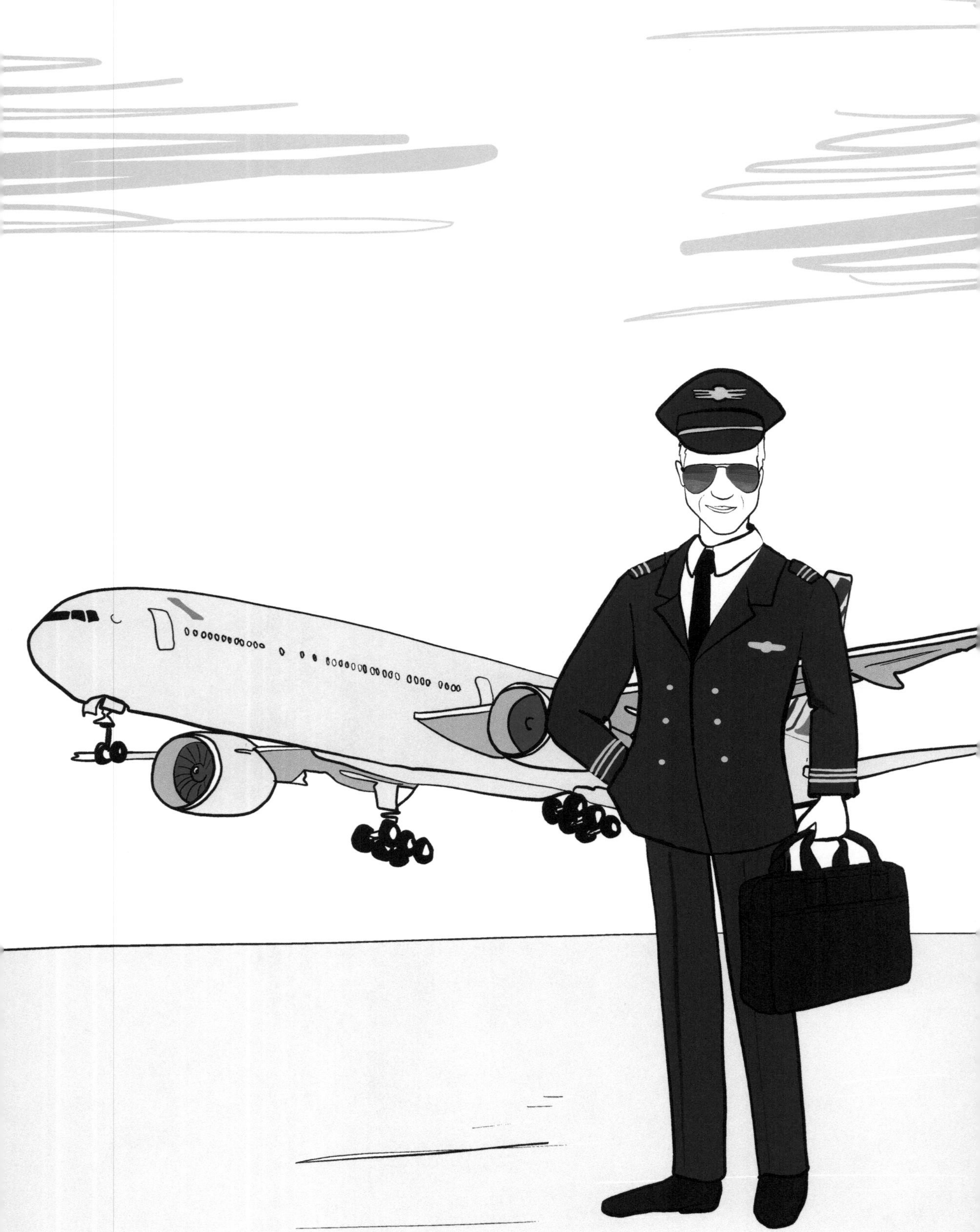

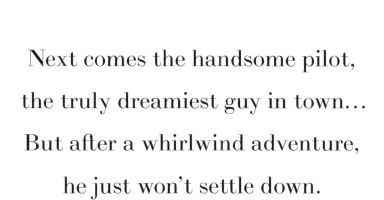

Next comes the handsome pilot,

the truly dreamiest guy in town…

But after a whirlwind adventure,

he just won't settle down.

There'll be artists filled with passion,

entrepreneurs with grandiose plans!

But for one reason or another,

Mr. Right seems impossible to land.

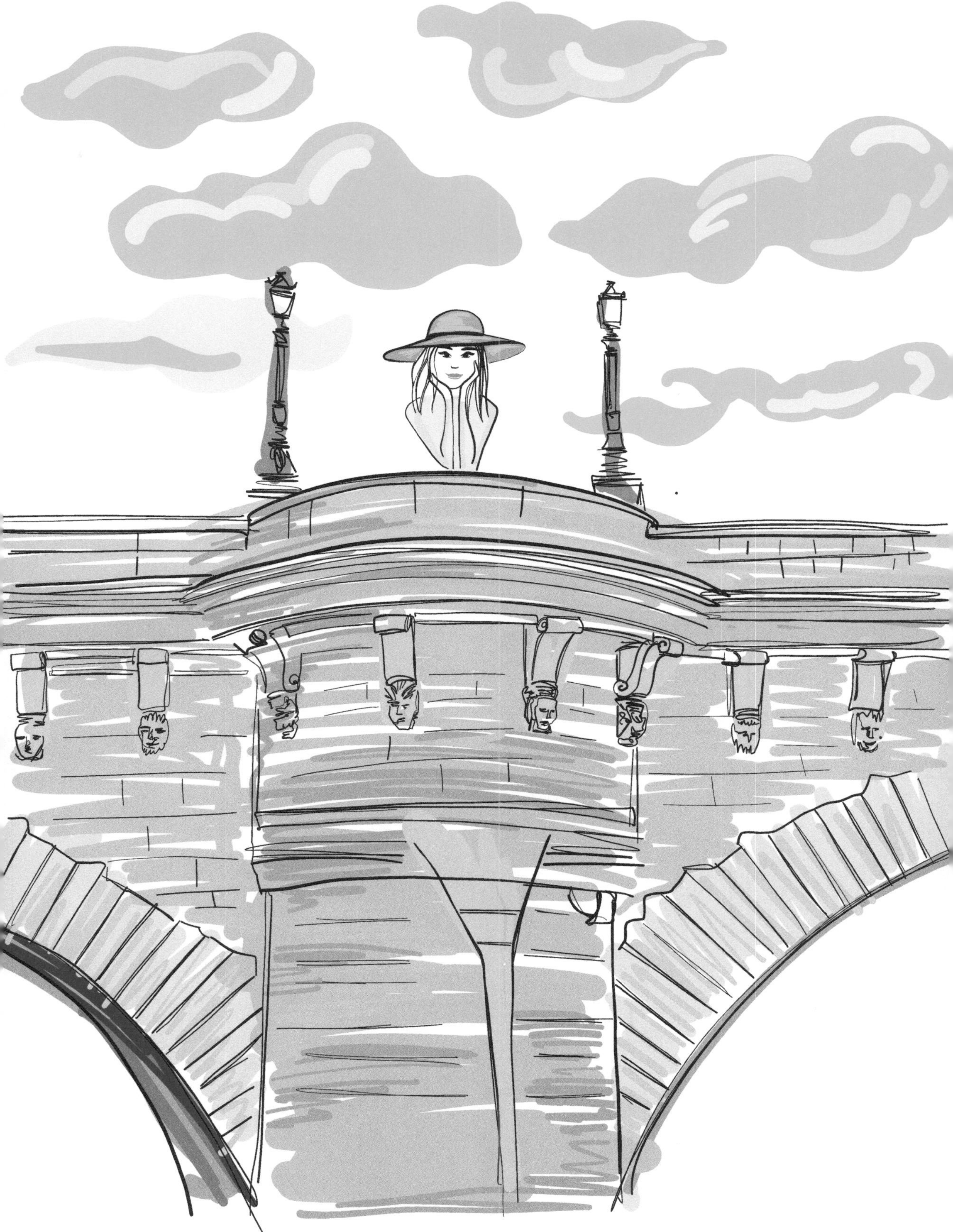

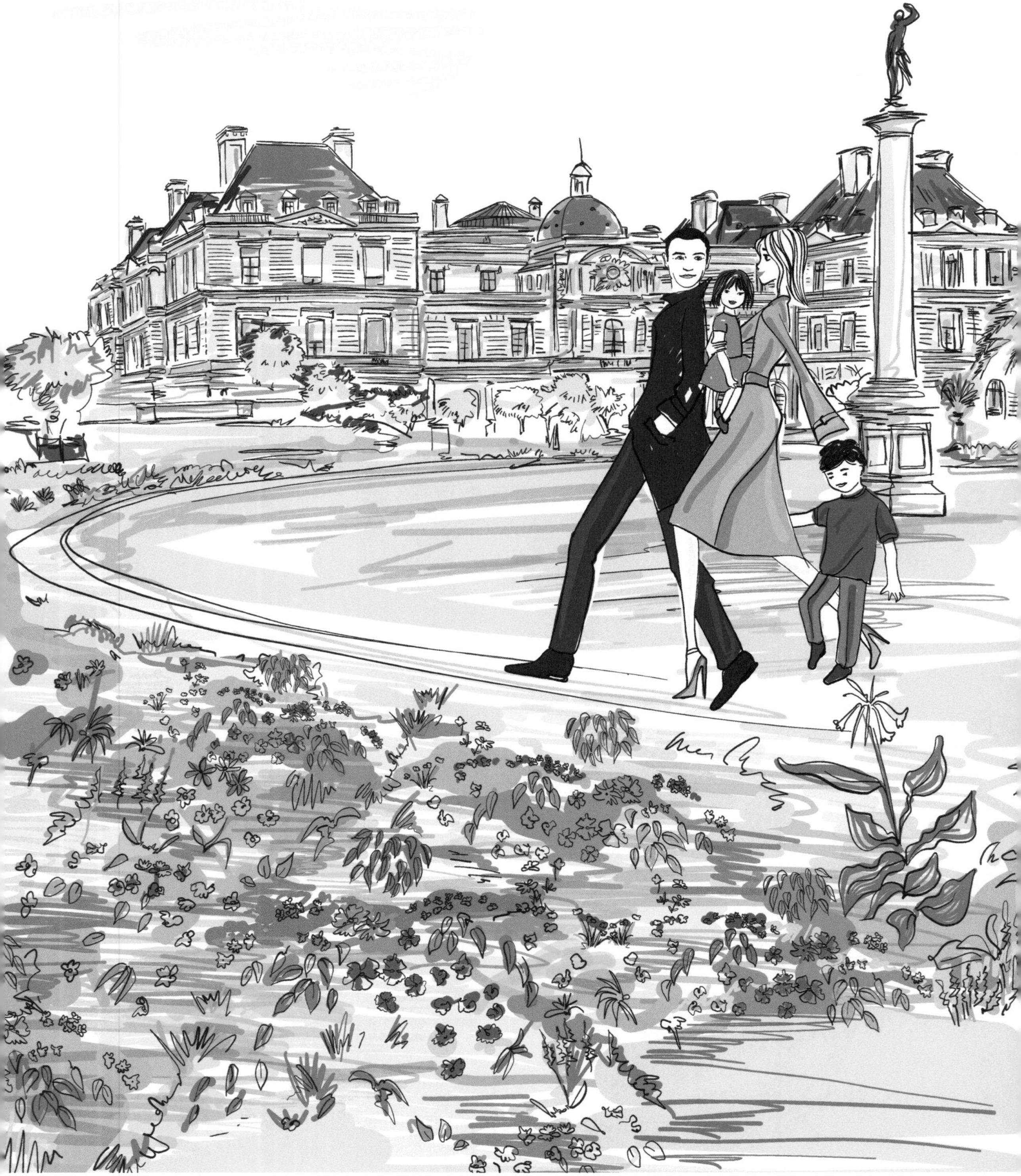

After what feels like a lifetime,
finally, you think you've found the one,
and you begin to envision your
future daughter and son.*

*Or whatever else your dreams entail

But just as you start to relish
in your ever-growing love,
he may suddenly get cold feet…
Making the sky crumble from above.

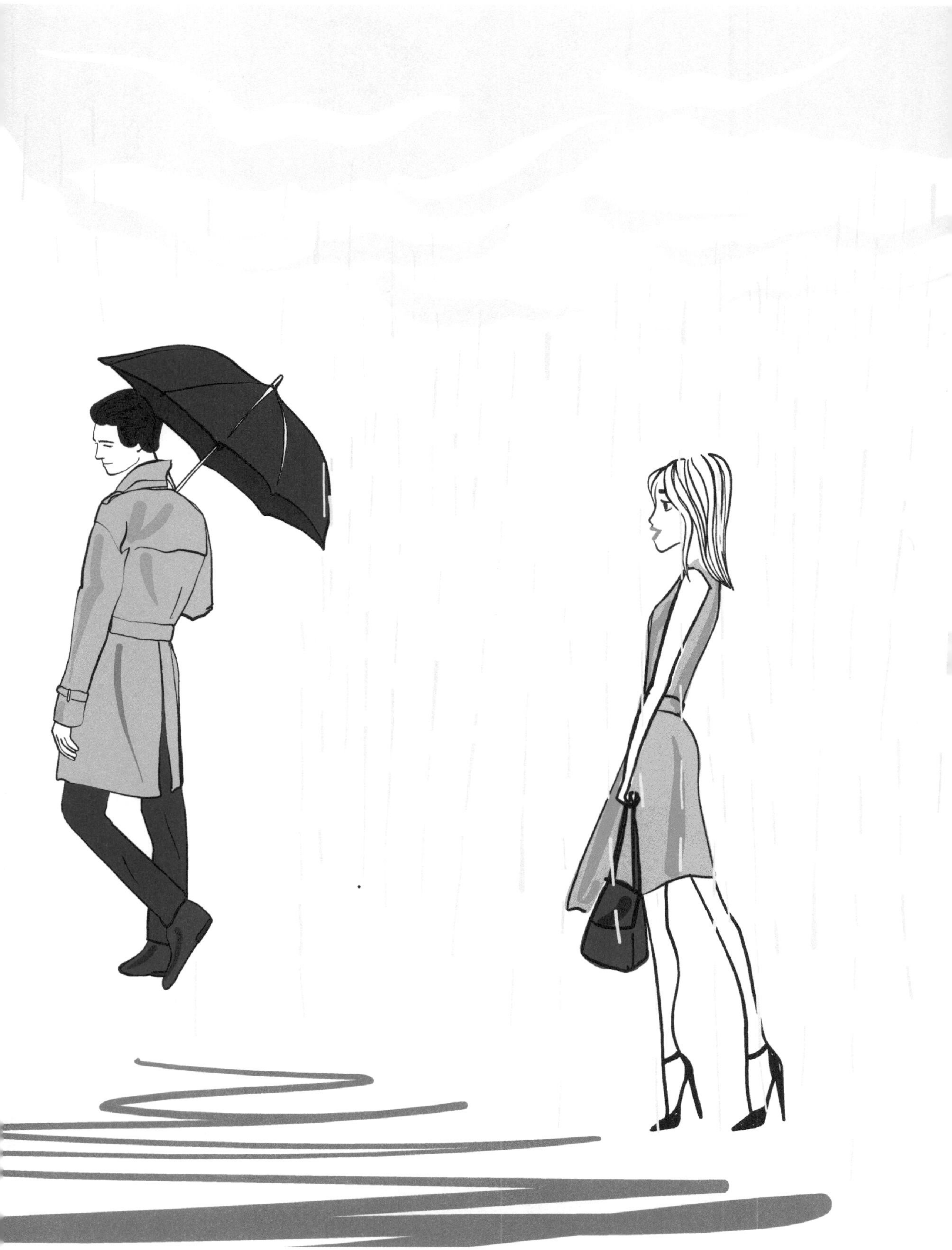

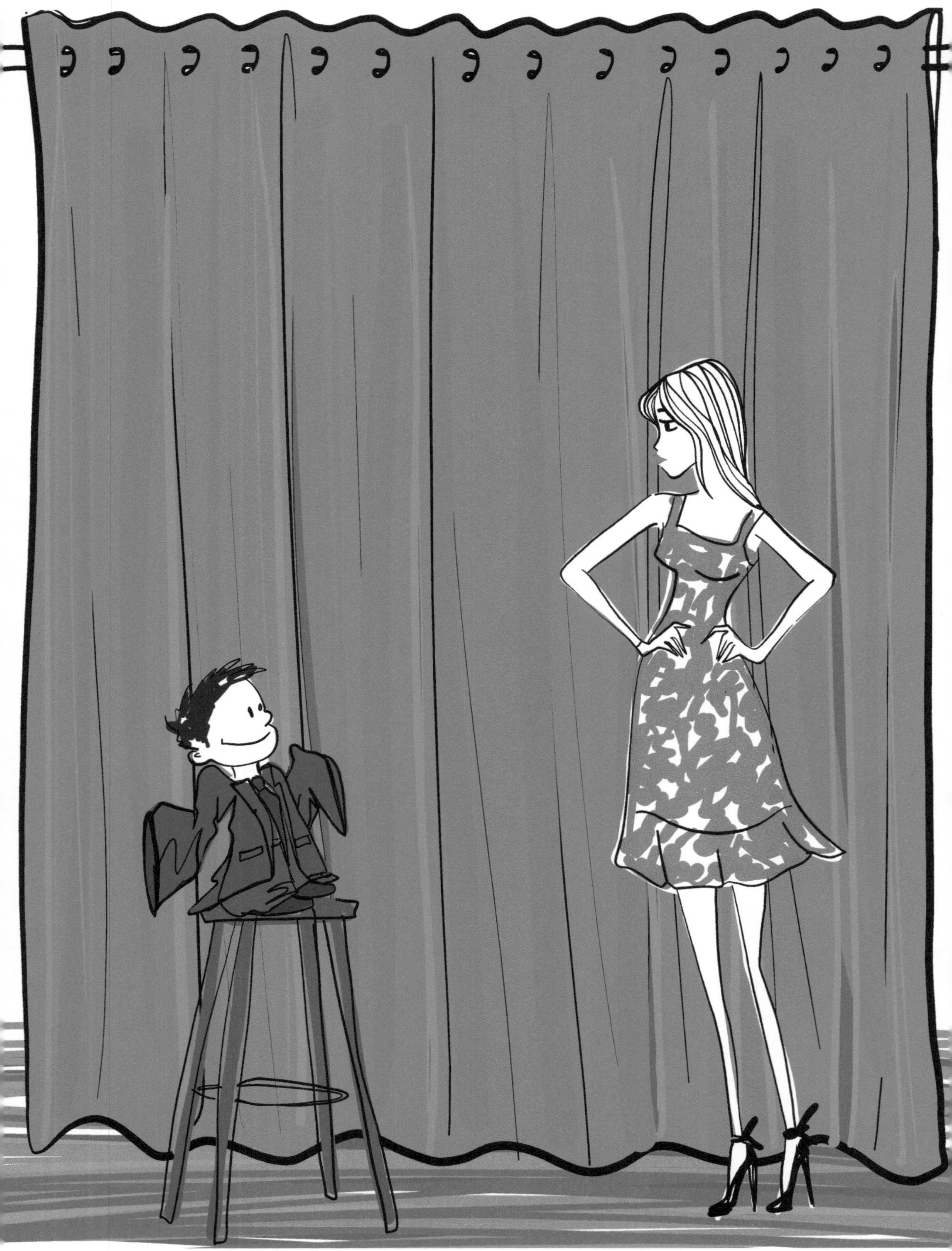

For regardless of his age,
he might not yet be a grown man.
And he may have as many fears
as any little boy can!

So he may crush your heart
and leave you feeling truly naïve.
But cheer up, sweet girl –
there's no need to grieve!

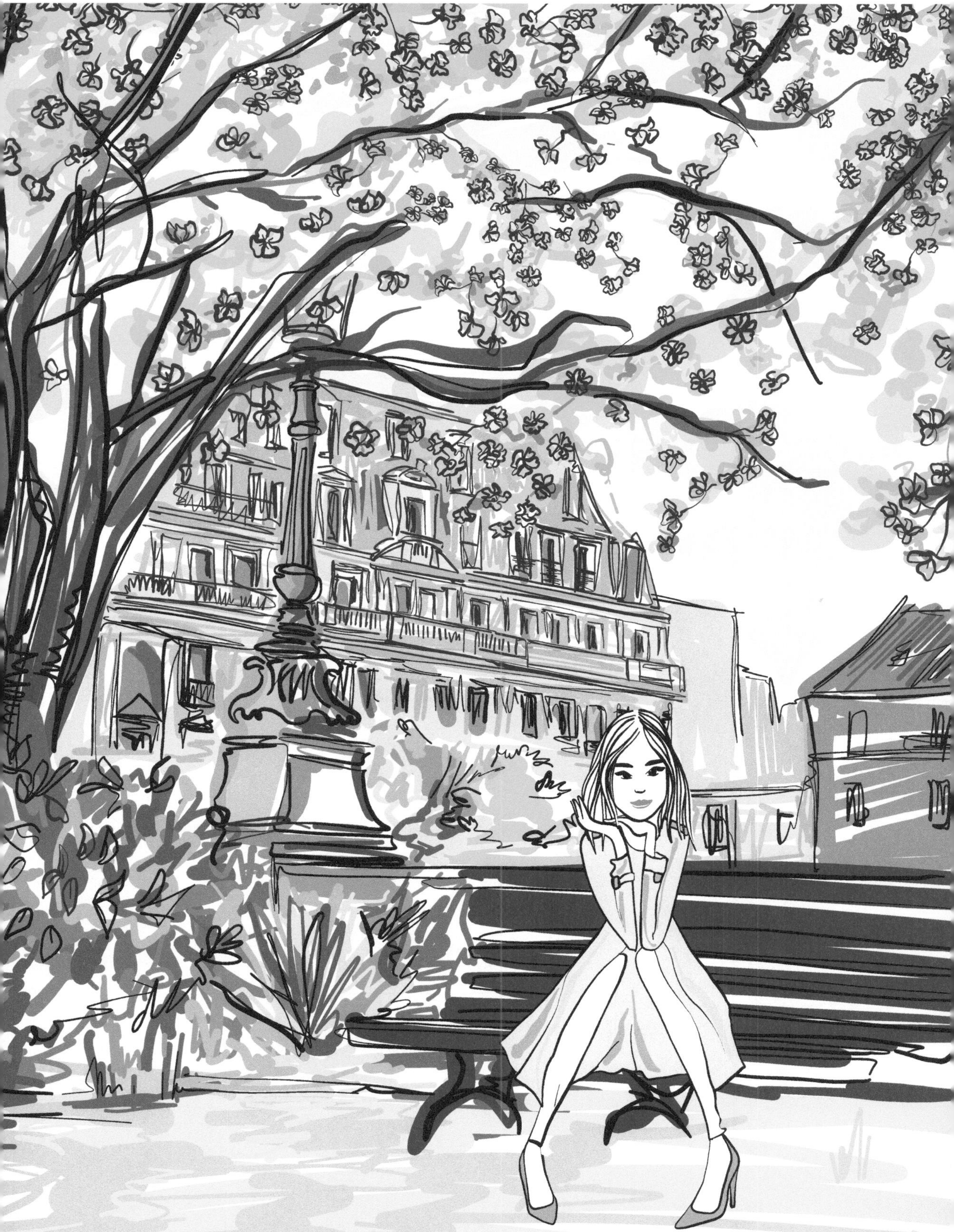

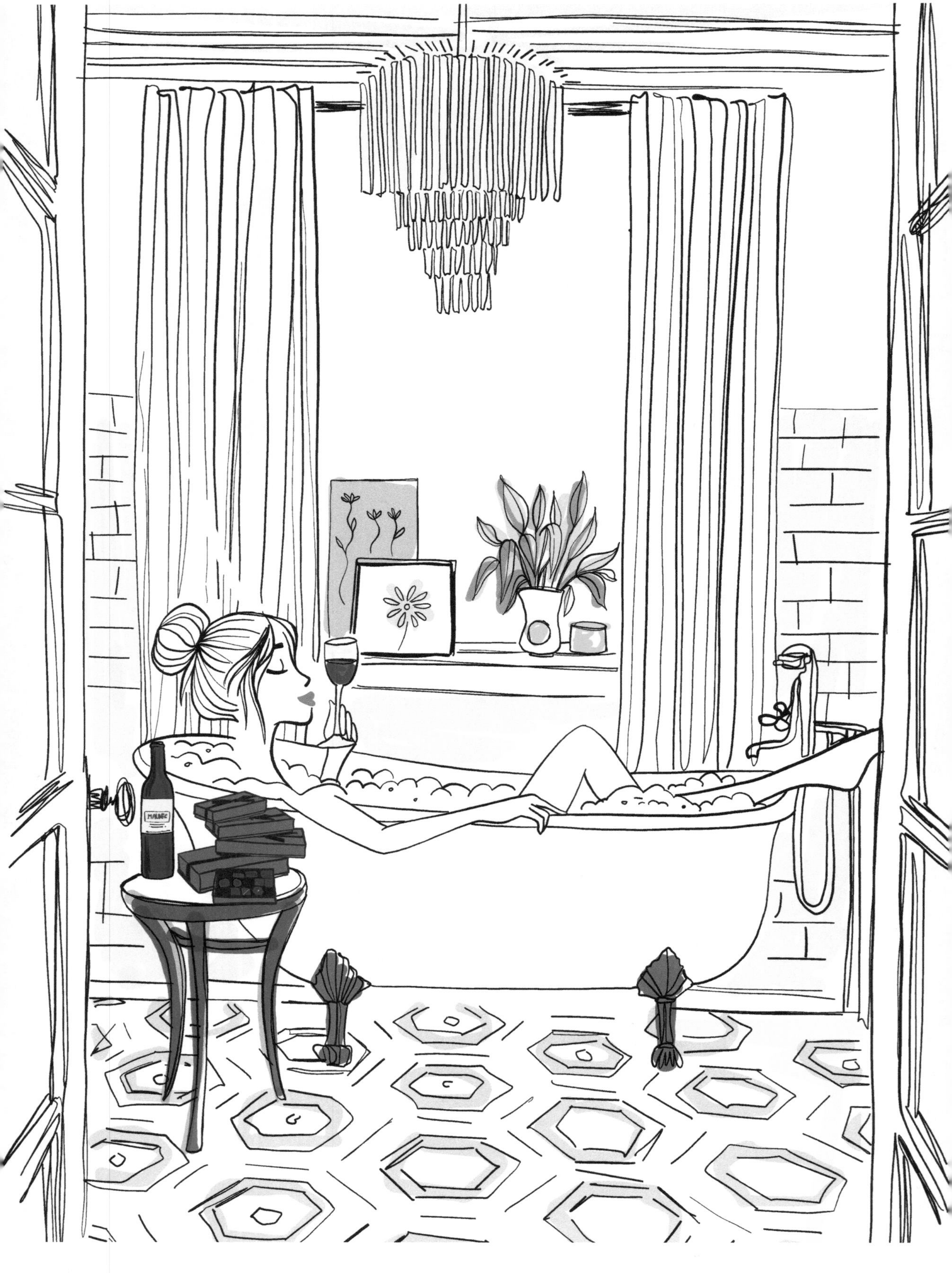
MALBEC

Sure, there'll be a few days of crying

and lots of chocolate and wine…

But the searing pain will subside –

just all in due time.

Then you'll brush yourself off
and hold your head high,
for no man is worth
the many tears you may cry.

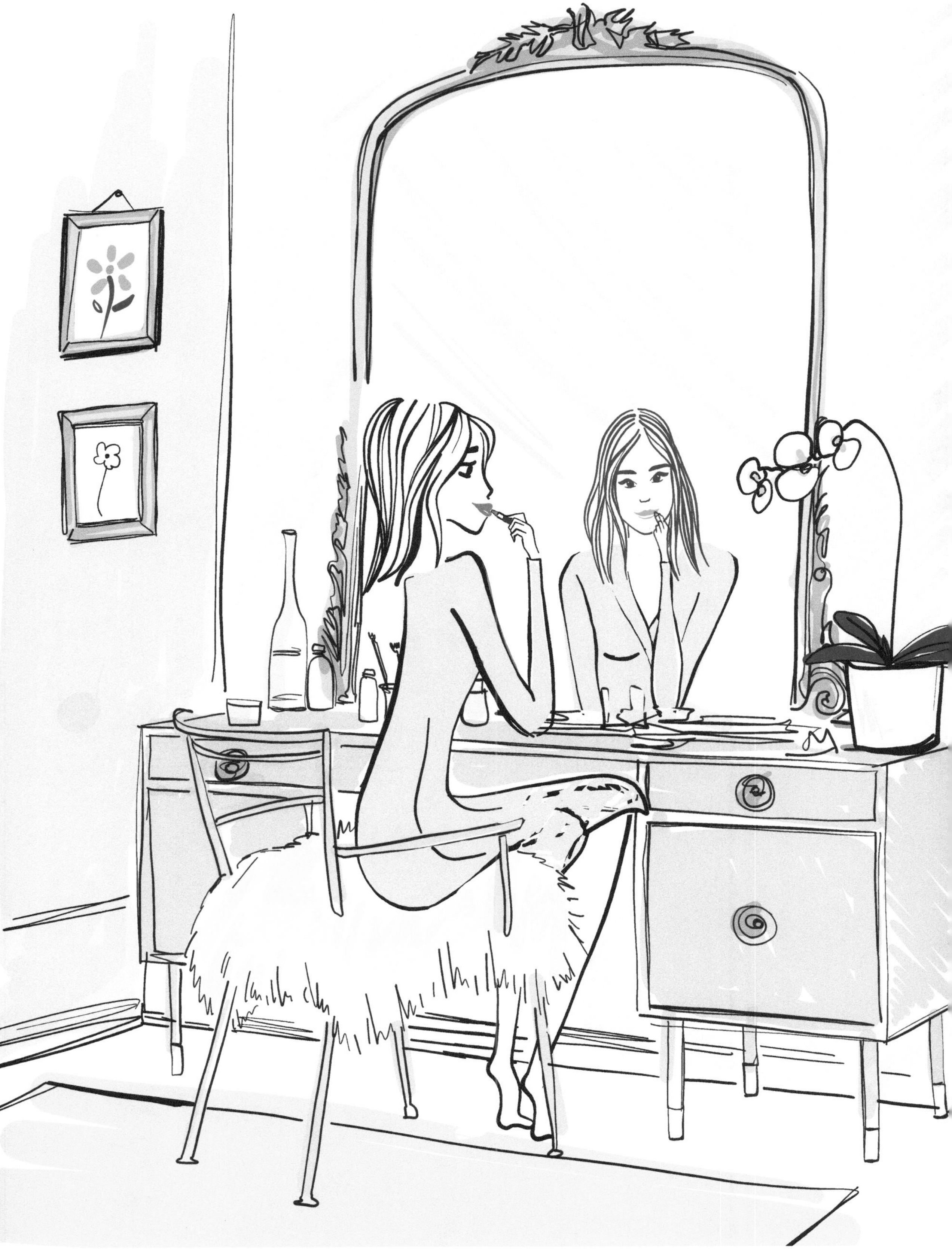

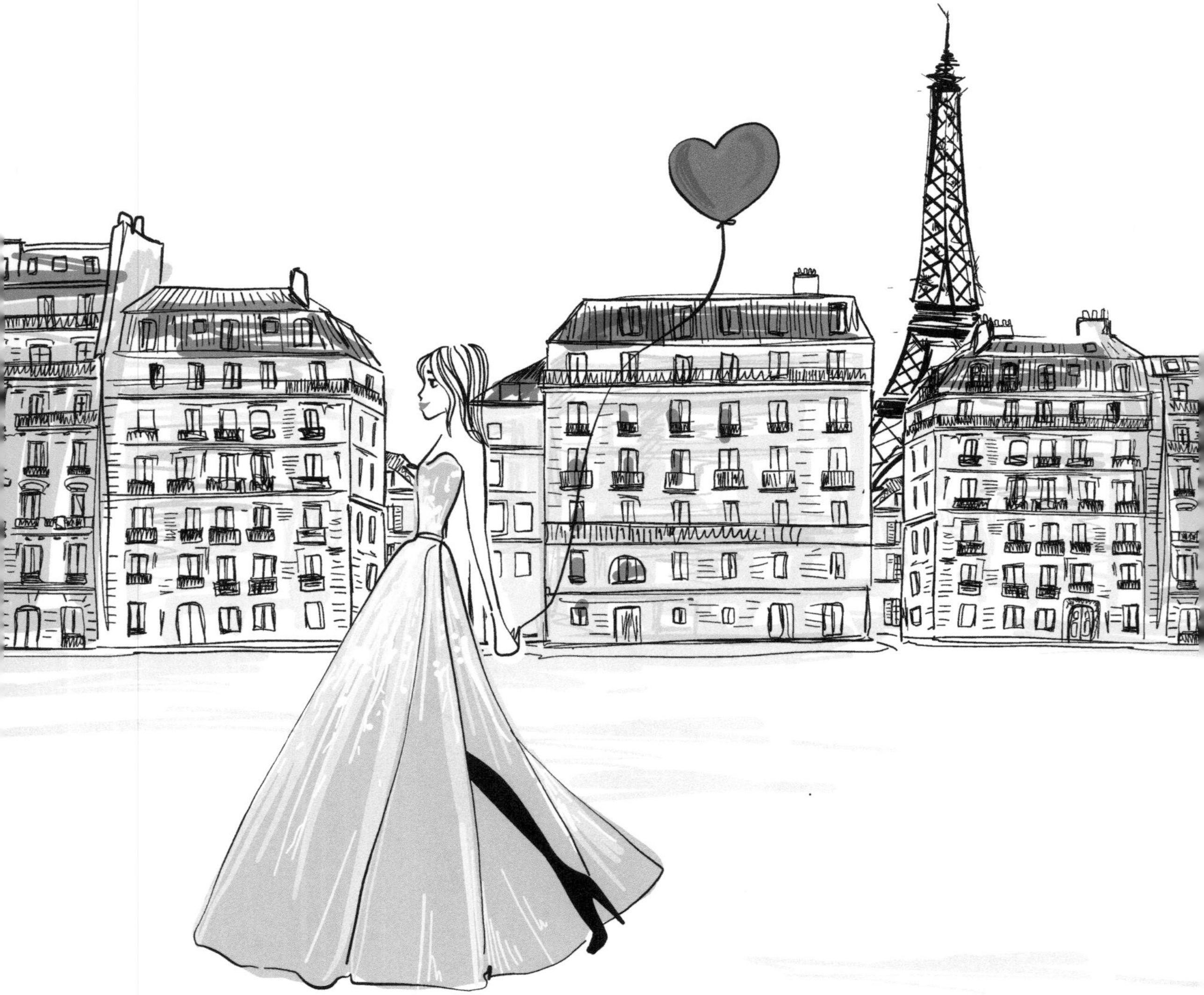

And so, on the quest for your

Prince Charming you'll proceed...

But in the process you'll discover

that you're already

**everything that you need.**

THE END

CPSIA information can be obtained
at www.ICGtesting.com
Printed in the USA
BVHW022152301119
565180BV00001B/1/P